nF420356

UpOn a Hill.

ON a HILL

---Part of the 'Kenyan Chronicles', Aug. 2024---

by

M. WEISGERBER

Sunset, skyset – every day there went forth that orb to both boil and die now, over the western hills, the slopes where both beauty and tales seemed to rise in earnest from those steep African hills. Chen stood there quite tired, feeling a little grizzled, looking up at where a mass of land and foliage rose further to the east, wondering again why he should be here, at this place, near this town, thinking of climbing such an insane peak as the sight that now lay ahead. The land here seemed made only of deep tree roots rolling on for a considerable way, grabbing, clutching, holding thick to his untested boots. Still time for a quick peek at the top though, a road beer, or even make it down to one of the nearby village clubs (at least before the town rolled its sidewalks up for the night).

Otherwise, he thought of his family's tune – the song's that could carry a feller through the day!

So he snapped some pictures of the locals as he went, debating his next course. For this was Muchakos, and though he wasn't here for long, he had been happy to find the poolside and nearby steep as charming as its inhabitants were intrepid, tall, youthful. Philippe, the matre'd had been right that this was a lovely walk; the thin air off the steepe more than made up for the lack of rum.

It had been hard enough to make it this far up the slope though in such a short time, as there had been several wonderous sights to distract him. The first had been a lovely rum garden carved out of some old townhouse on the lower flank, with views out over a small garden, of vineyards and coffee plantations flowing out away to the north. Then had been an actual *park* on the lower slope, with fascinating Kamba dancers, delightful Kamba drums, the Kenyan heat chasing away the last of the fleeting sun, with enough Kenyan reds and yellows and pinks and long legs to bewilder a mind. God, the girls were cute he thought, snapping a few pictures of the near women as much as the clouds now seeming directly at eye level, but also too a few shots of the cuter ones frolicking near.

One of the taller ones had noticed him though, flipping her hair against the curt watch of his brow, clearly suggesting to her friend in some form of Swahili that they move on. Damns, how his luck never seemed to hold! He did his best to try to ignore it, and her, but couldn't help but taste a bit of sting - best to go up then, move on.

Yet his legs had grown a bit tired wandering through the town all day, true, checking out the best of the village street stalls, nibbling on quality ugali, and wondering now that everyone seemed to be wearing hats, biceps and sharp insignias showing seeming everywhere. Yet his eyes had not grown tired of the sights, or the beauty shown around in a hundred unnamable forms that flowed around. The streetside plant nurseries, the colorfully clad locals. Steps and steps that spread out at all angles on the red earth, the shadow of a dragons back of the mountains rising high all around them.

Hell, even the graffiti around town was quite lovely, petering out as he rose, shifting minutely into imagery of gold, and beauty, and curvature everywhere, ceaselessly.

Oh how he loved sunsets too in these lush highlands; the turn of the colors upon the green, the rock – it was hard to realize he wasn't that far from either Nairobi nor Mombasa, that the fame of either could prelate this place (Muchakos, land of plenty, land of dreaming). He had missed seeing one of those lovely color sinks yesterday when he arrived, witnessing only the shades from the rental car depot, realizing far too late that it was well over a two-hour ride to the east side of the steep, let alone anything more. But not today. Though he was not much of a hiker, he was smitten by the little paths that branched ahead of him now, figuring that the best shot for a picture and the daydeath lay above, the greatest stories might lie somewhere there through the bows now gathering around him. He passed several large figurines made of mahogany as he rose, doing his best to click away as he passed. Best to keep moving though - now it was time for up, no more distractions, and to check another point off of the list. Passed where the graffiti lined even the bark of the nearest yellowwood trees.

The greatest change on this trip had been in the type of maps he read. Yes, there were the historgrams, the travel recommendations, the pictograms, all, certain to go along with hordes of attractive people bragging again and again seemingly only to themselves. Everywhere seemed to be murals and iconography, of arm and face paints of richly textured figures out wandering the grasslands, of long legs and wide rivers, but little that remained as truly curved, truly delightfully natural. Now however, as he trudged up the hill, he attempted to read the squiggle lines of topography, extrapolating upward and outward all the sideways lines cutting thickly across a page, he was struck by the beauty of the place. It had been a chore to learn the topo, sure, the curves that seemed at once familiar and yet totally obscene to his Liaoniese roots.

The hill in front of him had dozens of small switchbacks, almost invisible in the thickness of the brush.

Mlima. What a strange name for a hill — he would have to look into its history more later, but for now struggled with the steep quality of the paths, pushing past all the lounging locals and tourists on his way up up up. He had seen a vantage tower on both the tourist map and his mobile attraction map, and it looked quite promising, all told.   Another lovely spot to watch what was sure to be a spectacular sunset, and to add to his own collection of endless images for few hapless souls back home to click at, to possibly share, gain a bit of interest, intrigue. Behind him, he could see the shadows of the waders grow long, fingerlike.

Yet what was this?

CAILLIAC. A white stone at odds with the green and shadows rising all around, with one single word carved brazenly into its side, clean and uniquely polished. For a long moment he merely stood beside it, thinking how out of place it was with the reds of the soil, the unique greens of the brush after the morning drizzles. Gods though, he felt buzzed. Likely, it was just the first shifting of his locked muscles, or the rum, uncertain to things begging to be used. Yet the higher and higher he wandered, the more unusual the sights seemed to become. A giant cross of wood, double the height of a man emerging now off on the right.   Little playscapes, where children pranced nakedly. Graffiti fitting the best New York dens. A few fake tombstones, relics of the recent Halloween, rotten benches even, flat walls tilted at crazing angles.

Then this, now directly in front of him.

CAILLIAC. He wondered why this moniker should stand out to him, all in strait letters, seeming to look so very utterly Northern in its layout, its symmetry, so out of touch with the rhythm and sway of the lower folds he had wandered all morning. This one appeared carven on one of the cleaner stones, looking well cared for, except for this strange word or phrase that stood out of place to the greens and the darks all around. It looked like someone had tried to write the word 'Cadillac', or had goofed and then had given up halfway through. He started to wander on, doing his best to ignore it. There had been identical numerals painted on some of the bridges back in town he remembered, in similar goofy letters, or else partials maybe rubbed off. He snapped a few photos of this one, to check for a match, just in case, then headed still higher, flipping back. For some reason it spoke to him, almost vibrated in a manner similar to how the leggy girl had addressed him.

CAIL.

CAILLI.

(CAILLIAC?)

He shook his head, to clear himself. He had to keep going though, had to push a little harder if he was to catch the sunfall.

Still more up, then the tower, of course.

The tower! What kindness of Phillepe to suggest it, give meaning to the morning, and a direct & wearisome place to go.

"I don't know why they build," he had said, straitening his back as if to give a crack. "The locals quickly grew bored with it, and the tourista's seek and love only the beach.." So on he went, cursing his luck, cursing too the quality of the path that grew increasingly more tangled ahead of him..

Hell, now there was a bridge ahead of him! Always something, it seemed. It was an old thing, and had clearly been rotted out for quite some time. The main central ties had all collapsed from the frequent jungle rain, leaving only some metal, and some side supports in its place. It too was covered in the a similar graffiti that decorated the long boards in the town below. Hell, it even looked like these symbols were similar to some of the others throughout the town, him feeling a bit annoyed he hadn't noticed earlier. He flipped sideways through the reams and reams of pictograms that made up this sliver of his life – sure enough, similar patterns, twirls, runes. He looked again at his mobile, then up to the sky ahead, wondering what other challenges the gods might still throw at him, or if his luck might hold.

The hell with it. He clutched his pack a bit tighter, moving closer to the steel. He knew what Mei would have said, and thus started forward with a small smile before he knew what he was doing. He almost slipped twice as he threaded his way across, cut himself mildly on one of the neater struts, thinking of tetanus. He made it across with no real trouble though passed that first spell, and after pouring some rum on the wound, realized it wasn't much more than an abrasion after all.

Ah, there he was! After a bit longer than the map had shown, there was a burst of change. The trees had suddenly flown back, revealing a smooth grey partner amongst their midst. Ahead was the conical, tubular tower that bent in a way he almost recognized, all of shining steel, sharpened fingers of the edges plunging their sharp barbs up into the sky. Symbology had found these twigs too, but no matter - on all sides, the sundrenched land started to glow in a fever pitch of greens and reds.

A tower, how neat! So at odds with the sharp green and beetles scrurrying seemingly everywhere, the long tendrils of steel cutting dearly into the fell swoops and curves of the landscape.

He snapped more photos greedily, as he went up.

Ascending of the steps proved a chore, but worth the view. The city blossomed below him, little tendrils of streets and water falling away at all angles. The bright of the East Rift range too seemed all around, the island teeming as an inverted bowl to his tired mind. It looked stunning in the cooling of the eve, so pristine, and he wondered for a minute what would happen as fall truly fell on this land, little leaves giving way to sandy air. Again and again he snapped even more pictures, doing his best not to get too close to the edge, least anything happen.

Strange though; he had expected to see more people up here though, or else other photographers clicking way, having to jostle for the best view. The tower was lovely in a way that made it a picture man's dream, asymmetrical, with little side-booths where people could mingle, frolic, perhaps even kiss under the moonlight. Leave it to the local engineers to design something so beautiful as it was tall, yet all out of proportion with the human body though – it hurt his head just to look at it.

It looked like the sunset would be a bust, too, some long fingers of clouds seeming to come down from the north, a thick finger of stone threatening to obscure everything. He flipped back through the photos, admiring his own talent with a camera, the curves of the girls he had snapped earlier, letting his mind drift, letting his heart sway to the trill of the billion insects writhing round.

Boom.

He stood for a bit, mesmerized, the land sloshing out beneath him. Though he had heard the wine of some kind of flute music most of the way up here (Ndongu, he had to remind himself), yes the orutu again and again at times...yet this new sound almost sounded drum like. It even shook the tower a tad, its reverberations seeming to carry some cry, an energy, a charge calling out to the landscape seeming all around. His head began to swim at the thought, and he did his best to clear it with a swig from his canteen, of a passing of a hand across his brows.

(Oh, if only he had had some rum!)

Was this ground seismic he wondered? He recalled the rebuilding efforts in that had gone on on the near power plant stations from time to time, the ever haunting prospect of men digging for minerals, or geodes, or gold but had no idea here.

Better to be down, he guessed – better to be safe.

Probably, it was the altitude that made his head swim. Partly too, it was from all the bodies and attractive forms that had lined the way, or the curvature of the runescape below. Looking further, he tried his best to see through the twigs down to the park below.

Now though, all he could hear was his own simple heartbeat, his own ragged breath coming out in occasional sputters, spurts. And the reverberations of that boom going down and out towards the grasslands. What was it, had been exactly?

Maybe it was time for..

There it came again, sounding more threatening than the first: the thick of the Nyika landscape threaded away below him.

Boom boom: oh, how it made his head hurt, made him descend faster.

It was when he was about halfway down the tower that he realized what had nagged him at the summit. It hadn't been the light, nor the approaching clouds, but something so much closer to his lens that he hadn't been thinking about it, certainly not with his back mostly to the town. Back home, such a sight would have been covered with children, dog walkers, little people with snot clogging their faces. People would have been yelling obscenities, dealers in the corners stoned, looking for respite. Yet no humanly sounds could he here, no cough, sputter, or gaseous intake to humble him.

This was what triggered his thoughts on the way down.

He looked out and round, gasping at the sights he *could* see, checking his camera again, furiously. Though the angle was wrong, and he could only see a few of the northmost streets, the digital display proved him right.

What of the nearby village?

He peered closer into the camera histogram, expecting to see the thick tendrils of crowds milling about. People with jeeps had been lining the streets the entire day, farmers sailing their oxen as far out as they could into the green and red fields. It was the end of the work week, after all, and even with the heat of spring, and the thrill of vacationers, the streets below should have been jammed.

But no, the lens did not lie - they were suddenly all gone. White lights had begun to twinkle on it was true, casting ghost shadows where they fell, but the streets in his pictures were empty.   Everything around seemed frozen.

For a full minute, he thought himself cast back in time, looking at a dead place in the growing blue of the light before. Even the little river rivulets that crisscrossed the town seemed frozen. He was flipping again through his, debating about calling the hotel, back home, anywhere, but then the beats started up in earnest. Should he go up, above the treeline, to ensure the cameras accuracy? The validity of the thoughts streaming round?

No, no point. It was time to get down, time to forever get moving.

<hr>

He was just starting to get scared, just starting to feel the first slice of real fear sliding into him when he damn near ran into a Welshman, breathing out a sigh of relief. The forest around him had begun to grow quite dark beneath the canopy, the night noises coming through the overhead. He was thinking of going for his pocket torch, shocked at how dark the palm fronds made the twilight. Without warning though, he damn near ran into an old man standing silently, almost expectantly. He bounced off one of his shoulders, both annoyed and angry at the same time for the inconvenience, yet happy to see another human in all this waylaid green.

"Hey, sorry about that Mister," he tried, forgetting for a moment what a state, hell, which *country* he was on. He was dusting himself off, was reaching to offer the man a hand.

"You might want to run my good sir." The little fellow in front of him said, helping him up a tad, speaking softly in a language he did not at first fully understand.

"I, what?" Chen tried, yet a fell boom in the woods around him. They both looked at once toward the sound, which seemed everywhere and nowhere at once.

The old man ahead of him looked ashen faced now, his thin beard glistening with sweat. The ground moved a tad beneath them, drumbeats sure and true.

"I said, 'Time to run." The fellow even seemed to *smirk* as he said it, it was all so weird (meanwhile another *boom* rang out in the distance!) he wanted to ask, to question, but the old man was running back behind him, *up* the very slope, something glistening in his hand. Chen didn't wait to be told, fleeing back down, down, to what he knew not as the man scattered in another direction (did he run *into* the thick of the fray, carry his feet *toward* the drum sound?)

Ahead, the trail branched out again.

In his head, he could imagine fractals, spinning forever outward as his feet sailed over. He could see lines, processions coming round, but then, but then, something else. The very ground had begun to pulse, the dirt itself sweating sound. Left, right, turn (round).

For which way now was true down? The trails before him turned, squirmed around as living things, leaving his nerves a short fork twirling round. His feet caught, the ground itself threatening to opening up. Oh God, he could feel the pounding, pulsing coming up from the ground. The thrumming coming through the very air behind him. Something was coming then, was behind him, if he just twisted or turned he would be able to see them, would be able to feel sharp hands (or claws) beginning to wrap their way around his too-exposed neck..

The bridge! Oh, how he had forgotten of that stupid thing. In his head, all the little lines, and the trail had become so jumbled. A boom reached his ears, sounding neither of treefall, nor of firecrackers, wood splintering into the dusk. No, it sounded like a heartbeat from the very bowels of the earth, coming up to shake his toes, nose all. He was glad for an extra battery pack, happier still for his architectural memory of such twists and turns at this stage. Mei would have given him much crap for his forgetting, but he proved true.

Down he went, further onward.

CAILLIAC. He seemed to see the it everywhere now, little flakes and tendrils rising round, seeming to emanate from the very ground itself. It had been carved even into the steel frame of the bridge he saw, the very form of the bridge forming a giant letter "C".

He could hear it in the beat in the air.

He pushed himself faster over the bridge, pausing at the halfway before he realized what it was he heard amongst the song.

"Hello?" He paused for a second, looking back. He gave hope that it the old man, but recoiled when he saw the first. Someone was coming from back beyond, a long wave just visible in the darkness beneath the jungle trees. He leaned back, terror rearing back its ugly head.

"Hi!" said something below him, and he almost screamed as he looked down. The little ravine below was now filled with figures, most with wavery hair. Something about them looked mossy, ragged, and in moments they had started to ascend the very walls of the canyon.

The shadow before, the figures below: his only way of escape the uncertain yellowwood make of the bridge.

He ran flat out now, unsure of what to do, or where to go. His feet found footholds in the rot, seeming to bounce of the dusty and moonpitted landscape. He had gotten lucky that his memory of the place was apparently remained quite good, luckier still that the trail was easier here, the landmarks solid.

He could hear the little tinkle of laughter coming from between the trees, though, from the very bushes he passed on lefts and rights, gathering thick in the growing darkness. His hand, his very mind seemed to recoil from the true blackness of the shadows around. Left, right, down, down down. He didn't have time to check the map, everything becoming a blur. He thought he could see eyes, and forms of many curves approaching.

Their features all seemed slim, slanted, and he yelled at them to step back, step away.

CAILLIAC. Another sign passing, this one new, he was sure. An arm jutting out of the dark, from behind a tree, the same words cut into living flesh. Dodge, move, run. Run!

They were whispering, saying something behind him. Gaining, he was sure.

He tumbled back and back, feeling the first of the thick tree roots. He was up on his feet, seeing in his own head as the harpies, the wisps seemed to dance down the steep slope after him. He could hear sounds again, seeming far away, of a cello, of clapping, of a orutu's cry in the night. The trees below the bridge had seemed to be cast in white moonlight, though he remembered no orb as he ascended, what, half an hour, maybe an hour before. His hands were bleeding now, cut on the palm fronds smacking all around him. He waved his hands in front of his face, then was tumbling down, down, forever down.

Something was running down his hand now. He was thinking of Mei for some reason, the warm glow she could have given to a place, even a time like this.

He.

He burst forth into the park, into the main street of the town, tanned bodies suddenly everywhere around him, as if heeding his screams, his call. The sun *did* seem to have one last little trick, sliding out for a moment to turn everything bright reds and golds in the area around him, making him pause, making him fall. The effect on his tired eyes made them grow, made them luster. The familiar sodium lights were still blazing, still turning the figures approaching even stranger colors than they really were. At first he recoiled from them, seeing wide hands and gaping mouths that reminded him too much of the forest for first glance. Their faces were too dark, him forgetting that the sun was gone.

Yet then a large figure, a true Mzee, was jostling toward him, reaching for a kerchief. Then others too were nearing, a look of concern upon their brows. He waved again and again at them, but still the pressed onward.

As the townsfolk neared, he collapsed, looking up at the strange sky that wheeled overhead, listening only to the fading voices, the gasps of the townsfolk as the pointed, gasped.

"There's something....something up...on the hill..." he tried, looking up, far too up into the nearest face that approached him, realizing too late that they might be here to help. In his rush he had forgotten what little Swahili, English, anything could help him, resorting back to the plainspeak of points and grunts to guide him.

The sky was different though, stronger down here, where the same constellations seemed meaningless under a darkened sky. The Mzee looked down at him, then up to the peak, where he (she?) made a sign to themselves.

(Don't go out a wandering, don't a go a...)

Cold, so cold he thought, turning down, turning inward.

Above, true night drifted in.

Mlima: such a strange name, he thought to himself...

(Meanwhile, local laypeople did their best not to stair too long out their windows, at the sight now filling the street..)

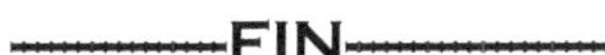
FIN

SISTER STORIES

(Being of the PACIFIC NW Series)

-**OCCIDENTALE LOCALE, E** (2019)

-Cascadia, Redefined (2019)

-**SEALTH, THAT SNEAKY CIT** (2020)

-Death on Discovery Pointe (2014)

-***THAT* MAN** (2019)

-Alpine Madness (2020)

-**RUNAWAY ON 12TH STREET BRIDGE** (2020)

-Lost on Eastlake (2021)

-That House on Denny Way (2021)

-**LOST ON EASTLAKE** (2022)

-The Fountain (2022)

-Bending North (2022)

-**HOH** (2022)

-Blosso*m* (2022)

ABOUT THE AUTHOR

("What doth a humbled mind seekth?")

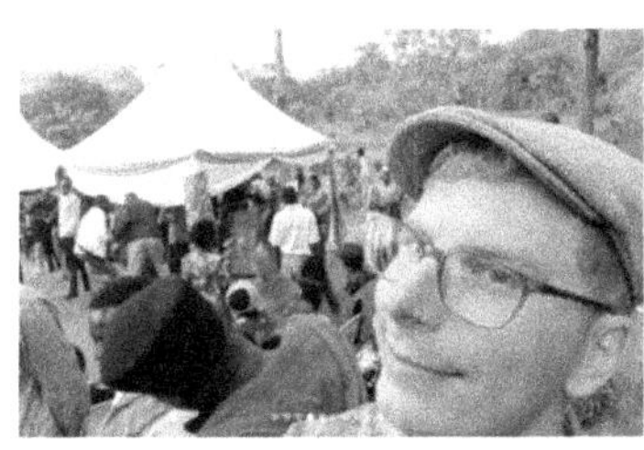

M.Weisgerber is a sustainable architect from the Pacific
Northwest (and sometimes Detroit) who spends his non-
design hours & evenings immersed in the theatrical world of
writing & literature. He first had a chance to visit Kenya for
the first time in 2023, being deeply moved by its people, its
culture, and the overall kindness experienced by everyone he
encountered. He looks forward to writing more about his
wanderings and adventures and visiting in that stellar land
again soon (and perhaps getting to Mombasa in the sun!), and
misses the local tea & ugali dearly under eternal summer sun..

He currently lives in the Tenas Chuck
watershed with his cat KB, and can be
found wandering along the muddy
quaysides of the Salish Sea on all the off
days.

His doodles & other works can also be found at:

www.maweisg.com   &   **ig: m.weisswrites**